CONTENTS

Introduction

Building is one of the oldest human activities of all. Our very earliest ancestors lived in Africa, where the hot climate probably meant that they could make do with only the simplest of shelters. As soon as people began to explore new lands and move northwards, however, they needed to protect themselves from the cold by building homes.

To start with, people used whatever materials they could find to make their houses. Where there were trees, wood made an ideal building material. In other places, such as the Middle East, people worked out how to make bricks from mud. These early builders also learned to make their houses suit local conditions, for example, by building their homes on stilts in places that flooded regularly.

By the time of the ancient Egyptians, around 5,000 years ago, people were building in stone. Stone is a heavy material, difficult to carry and work, but it is durable and lasts for centuries. So people like the Egyptians and the Maya of Central America made their most important buildings out of stone – especially their temples and pyramids. Other ancient peoples, such as the Greeks, also used stone for temples.

IDEAS AND INVENTIONS

BUILDING A WORLD

Innovations in Construction Techniques

Philip Wilkinson

Illustrated by Robert Ingpen

Chrysalis Children's Books

First published in the UK in 2005 by
Chrysalis Children's Books
An imprint of Chrysalis Books Group Plc,
The Chrysalis Building, Bramley Road, London W10 6SP

ISBN   1 84458 214 0

British Library Cataloguing in Publication Data
for this book is available from the British Library.

Editorial Manager: Joyce Bentley
Senior Editor: Rasha Elsaeed
Series Editor: Jon Richards
Editorial Assistant: Camilla Lloyd
Designed by: Tall Tree Ltd
Cover Make-up: Wladek Szechter

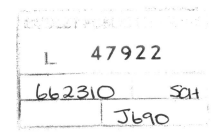

Previously published in four volumes for Dragon's World *Caves to Cathedrals, Science & Power, Scrolls to Computers* and *Wheels to Rockets.*

Printed in China

10 9 8 7 6 5 4 3 2 1

The Romans went further, developing concrete, which enabled them to design buildings with curves; they became experts at building domes and vaults.

So one of the most modern building materials, concrete, was actually developed over 1,000 years ago by the Romans. These inventive people did not stop there. They also built major roads and founded some of our most important cities, from York to London.

Another building technique used widely today, making a metal frame to hold up a tall building, was also developed long ago, by the ironmasters of the eighteenth and nineteenth centuries. Nineteenth-century builders developed iron and steel frames to put up amazing structures like London's Crystal Palace and the Eiffel Tower in Paris. When they realized that metal frames were ideal to support factories and office blocks, too, the skyscraper was born.

Without the work of these early builders, the modern buildings that fill our cities today would be impossible. Our office blocks, schools, factories, hotels and shopping malls, although they may have twenty-first century 'skins', are actually supported by steel 'skeletons' similar to those first built by the great engineers of the nineteenth century.

PHILIP WILKINSON

SHELTER & REFUGE

The first people relied on caves or trees to keep them warm and to protect them from wild animals as they slept, but, gradually, people learned to construct shelters from materials that they found around them.

A s early people migrated to cooler northern climates, they found that they needed a place where they could keep warm and be safe from wild animals while they slept at night. A cave could form a strong natural refuge, and early people certainly did use caves for shelter, as the remains of bones, tools and early graves in hilly regions of France, Spain and Germany show. However, as people slowly spread to many parts of the world where there were no caves, they needed to find other ways of sheltering from the elements.

BUILDING WITH WOOD

Early people must have been able to build simple shelters. These temporary shelters would have been built from materials that people found around them. Perhaps the early hunters simply broke branches off trees and leant them against a rock to form a low shelter they could crawl under to sleep.

△ *A cave provided natural shelter and also protected the fire from the weather.*

▷ *Huts or tents grouped together in a circle gave added protection from wild animals and from the weather.*

EARLY ARCHITECTURE

Early houses came in a variety of shapes and sizes. At Khiroktia in Cyprus, people built round, domed houses like beehives. Houses in Mesopotamia were usually rectangular and built around a courtyard, but there were also 'tholoi' or circular houses. These strange buildings had a rectangular roofed section with a circular, domed room at one end. At Catal Hüyük, there were no streets between the houses. People got about by crossing the rooftops. The doors into the houses were in the roof. Each house had a room set aside as a shrine, a storeroom and a living room with built-in benches and platforms for sleeping, sitting and working on.

Many towns were built with houses crammed together and narrow, winding streets. The towns were often surrounded by a wall to keep out invaders. Jericho, the world's oldest town, was enclosed by a stone wall three metres thick.

Mohenjo-Daro and Harappa in Pakistan were two of the first cities to be laid out on a grid system. The main streets ran in straight lines from north to south. Smaller lanes crossed them from east to west.

Although these shelters disappeared long ago, there are some clues to help piece together a picture of early shelters. The site of a settlement dating back at least 125,000 years has been found at Terra Amata in southern France. Archaeologists have identified holes in the ground where poles were stuck into the soil to make the framework of huts, and the outlines of stones which must have been used to weigh the poles down. Studies of huts made by modern hunter-gatherers such as the Bushmen in Africa help archaeologists to work out what these ancient huts were like.

BUILDING WITHOUT WOOD

It was not so easy to make shelters in the icy wastes of the northern lands, where building material was scarce. As hunters followed mammoths on to the vast, open steppes in Russia and Siberia, they found a bleak landscape whipped by icy winds, where hardly any trees grew. The answer was to build huts from the remains of the mammoths they had killed. The circular wall of the hut was made from stones and large bones, packed with mud. The roof was made of small branches or smaller bones and reindeer antlers.

Shelters could also be made by weaving branches together to form two screens and then leaning them against each other. A screen of branches curved round in a cone became a hut. A framework of long sticks stuck into the ground or weighed down with stones would hold the hut upright. The sticks could be tied together with creepers or grasses, leaving a small gap for a door. Then, more branches could be woven in, or the hut could be covered with grass, leaves or skins.

6

1

2

3

4

5

Shelters were made from whatever material was easily available. The early farmers of the Middle East built mud brick houses (1). Wattle and daub huts (2) were common, made by plastering woven branches with mud. Where there was a danger of flooding, people built houses on stilts (3). Nomads made tents from skins (4 & 5). In the north, mammoth bones were used to build strong huts (6).

SHELTER AROUND THE WORLD

People have always adapted their houses to the climate they live in and the materials around them. Around the world, many of these traditional methods of building still survive today.

 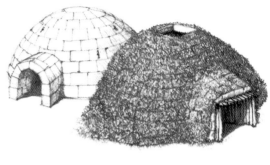

The Inuit are hunters who live in the frozen Arctic regions of North America and Greenland. In the winter, when it is very cold and there is hardly any sunlight, the traditional Inuit shelter was the igloo, built from large blocks of ice. In summer, they lived in shelters roofed in turf.

The nomadic peoples of North America followed the migrations of herds of bison across the plains. They used wooden poles and animal skins to make tents. Some made cone-shaped tents, known as tepees. They could be laced up to keep out the bitter winter cold. Others made round huts covered with skins.

 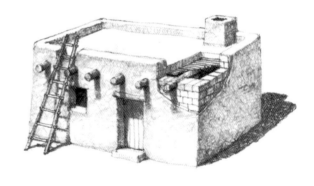

In the Middle East, the weather is much the same all the year round. The days are hot and the nights are cold. Early farmers built houses of mud bricks with flat roofs. The roof was supported by wooden rafters. In some places, houses like these are still common.

In the tropics, it is hot and humid all the year round. There is heavy rain nearly every day and rivers and lakes sometimes flood. Early people in these regions fished and farmed. They built houses on stilts to keep the floor above flood level. The frame was wood and the walls and roof were thatched.

Tents made from animal hides on a wooden or bone framework probably provided many early shelters. Archaeologists have discovered evidence in Germany which shows how reindeer-hunters made their tents about 15,000 years ago. By this time, the ice was beginning to melt, leaving tundra where reindeer grazed. Reindeer moved faster than mammoths, and hunters had to kill more animals to provide enough meat. The hunters moved on every few days, following the herds north in the spring and south in the autumn.

PORTABLE HOMES

The hunters could never be sure of finding shelter on the bleak tundra, so they devised the tent, a home that was light enough to carry around and quick and easy to set up at the new camp. These tents had a simple cone-shaped framework of poles tied together at the top. The frame was covered with a layer of reindeer skins. If the ground was too hard to dig the poles into the soil, the hunters could weigh the framework down with stones. Some hunters secured the tents with ropes. Ropes made from animal sinew or other flexible material were stretched out from the top of the tent and tied round stones on the ground. In winter, the hunters built a wall of stone or sand around the base to give the tent extra protection against the icy wind. They also built a small fire inside the tent to keep themselves warm.

THE END OF THE ICE AGE

As the climate continued to change and people no longer had to migrate, the need for portable tents was not so great. The weather was warmer and the new forests provided plenty of material for making shelters quickly and easily. It was not

△ *Branches were lashed together with creepers.*

necessary to drag poles and skins around, as hunters could cut wood and make shelters wherever they happened to stop. Making tents from skins had meant that hunters had to kill large animals, and there were fewer of these animals around at this time.

There were disadvantages in making temporary shelters each time they settled in a new place. The frame had to be made from long, straight poles which could be difficult to find. It was hard work chopping the wood and trimming off branches with a primitive stone axe. The shelters would probably have been very small and low, and not very comfortable to sleep in. Building a low wall to support the poles or building the hut over a shallow pit gave a bit more height, but the shelters were still not ideal. The biggest disadvantage was that these lightweight shelters did not give much protection against any predators.

SETTLERS

By 6000 BC, people who still lived by hunting and gathering tended to stay in one place for long periods, catching fish or hunting deer. They would chop down trees to make a clearing in the forest and build huts that were bigger and stronger than earlier shelters.

A settlement at Lepenski Vir on the River Danube in Serbia had wooden huts which were shaped like ridge tents. Long, strong poles were leaned against each other in an upside-down V-shape, probably with a fork at the top to hold the long ridge pole. The roofs would have been thatched.

People living in China also built fairly substantial wooden houses from about 5000 BC. Houses at Pan P'o Ts'un had thatched roofs made of reeds and straw. The roof was supported on wooden poles inside the house. The houses were often round with walls of 'wattle and daub', which is made by weaving branches together and plastering them with clay to

△ *Reeds made a useful thatching material.*

give a solid surface. The Chinese also made rectangular houses with a thatched roof that sloped right down to the ground. A pit was dug in the floor to give headroom inside the house.

MUD-BRICK HOUSES

When people settled down in communities, they began to build more permanent houses. Houses were still made of wood in places where there were plenty of trees. However, trees were scarce in the areas where farming began, so early farmers had to find another way of making shelters.

People living in Mesopotamia, India and lands around the eastern Mediterranean learned to make their houses from mud bricks or 'adobe'. They noticed that mud is soft and sticky when it is wet but that it bakes hard in the hot sun. If the mud could be moulded into a suitable shape, they could use it to build a wall. To build a wall, the dried mud bricks were laid one on top of the other and stuck together with mortar made from mud. When the building was finished, the outside was plastered with more mud to give extra protection from the weather.

CHANGING SHAPE

Many early houses were round like tents, but, gradually, people began to build rectangular houses. This was more suitable for fitting the buildings together in a settlement. There was not much rain in these regions so the roofs were flat, or sometimes thatched with reeds.

These early brick houses lasted for a long time, and there are still many mud-brick buildings in the Middle East, some of which are thousands of years old. The modern system of making bricks is really only a more sophisticated version of baking clay until it is hard.

MUD BRICKS

At first, mud bricks were shaped by hand but this was laborious and it was not possible to make regular shapes. So the early builders began to press mud into rectangular wooden moulds, ramming it down hard into the corners to get a sharp edge. The bricks were left to dry in the sun or baked in an oven. The first bricks were not very successful because the mud cracked as it dried but this problem was solved by adding straw.

ROADS

Fine roads were built by the Persians, the Chinese and the Romans. Later in history, a journey by road became a nightmare for travellers who had to face rocks, potholes, mud and floods.

The first people on Earth lived by hunting and gathering food, roaming from one place to another in search of food and shelter. They had not yet begun to cultivate the land, to keep animals or to live together in communities. Their movements were haphazard, and they tended to avoid places where other people might have been searching for food before them. There was no need for roads or even for simple tracks to take people from one place to another.

TRADE AND TRAVEL

All this changed once people settled down, grew crops and raised livestock. They began to trade, exchanging their surplus farm produce for other goods. Some people specialised in crafts such as making pots, carpentry or metalwork, and they often set up their businesses in

△ *The Persian Royal Road, built about 3500 BC, was used by the army to move quickly around the empire to put down uprisings and rebellions.*

▷ *The Romans built a network of roads around their empire. The roads were so strong and thick, they were more like underground walls.*

14

villages and towns. These developments created the need to travel, and the need for tracks running between settlements.

These early tracks were paths worn across the landscape by traders and their pack animals. They developed into recognized routes because they avoided obstacles such as mountains or difficult river crossings. Travellers usually chose open country where they were less likely to be attacked by wild animals or hostile tribes, so many tracks ran along ridges or across open desert.

MILITARY ROADS

The ancient civilizations of the Middle East were the first to turn these rough tracks into roads. There were roads connecting Babylon and Egypt, and linking such cities as Assur and Babylon. Parts of these roads, dating from about 700 BC, have survived. In some ways, they were surprisingly modern in the way they were made. A foundation of rubble and gravel was covered with a layer of bricks and the road surface was made of stone slabs. They were built to last.

As the great empires of the ancient world expanded, their rulers built roads so that they could communicate more easily with their more distant regions. Although they were often used by traders, roads were built mainly for use by soldiers. The Persian Royal Road, built round about 3500 BC and in use until about 300 BC, was one of these. It was a network of roads which ran from Susa on the Persian Gulf to places such as

Milestones were placed along Roman roads so that the army could tell how far it had travelled.

Jerusalem, Nineveh and the Black Sea. The empires of China, Egypt, ancient Greece and the Incas of South America also had their road networks, built by slaves.

ROMAN ROAD-BUILDERS

The Romans brought road-building to a fine art. Their network spread out from Rome across their empire, north to south through Italy, France and Spain, and eastwards to Turkey. After the Romans invaded Britain in 54 BC, they created roads which until recently formed the country's major road network.

The roads of the Roman empire covered about 85,000 kilometres. They were built mainly to link the army garrisons which controlled the provinces. If trouble broke out, more troops could quickly be brought in to take charge. To help troop commanders check that they had marched the right distance each day, the Romans placed milestones by the side of their roads.

The Romans were expert engineers and surveyors. This enabled them to build their roads straight except where it was necessary to avoid an obstruction. The high point of their road-building was the Appian Way, the great military road leading to Rome. In some places, the foundations were 1.5 metres deep.

Building began by digging a deep trench. A layer of sand or mortar was placed at the bottom, and large, flat stones were laid on top. Then came a layer of smaller stones mixed with lime, a layer of gravel and coarse sand mixed with lime, and finally a top surface of volcanic lava.

Like all Roman roads, the Appian Way was curved or 'cambered', so that rainwater would flow away.

THE DISAPPEARING ROADS

By AD 400, the Roman empire was divided and in decline. The roads that the Romans had left behind in Europe gradually deteriorated for lack of maintenance, and in many places they disappeared altogether.

The people of the Middle Ages had little use for roads. They relied mainly on horses and pack animals, which could use the older hilltop tracks, rather than on wheeled vehicles. As towns and cities grew in size from about 1500 onwards, the need for communication and trade increased. At this time, a journey of any length at all in a wheeled vehicle must have been very difficult. Cartwheels made deep ruts in winter, and the hooves of the

THE ROAD TO EMPIRE

Most road-building in the ancient world was for military use. As empires expanded, rulers needed to ensure that their armies could move about with ease.

The roads built by the ancient Chinese were designed for use by marching soldiers. In mountainous areas, they included flights of stone steps.

The Romans' roads, too, were for use by the army. They were planned to allow columns of soldiers to march side by side in fours without breaking ranks.

Military road-building continued until recent times. In the eighteenth century, the English army built roads in Scotland to control rebellious Scottish clans.

After the fall of the Roman Empire, the surface of many Roman roads deteriorated gradually. As the roads fell into disrepair, they were not used so much.

animals pulling them churned the tracks into seas of mud. Potholes appeared where stones had been washed away by storms. It is not surprising that a journey of more than a few kilometres was thought of as a dangerous adventure, and few people travelled at all except in the summer months.

PAY AS YOU GO

Communities were encouraged to maintain good roads in their own areas, but not all of them did so. In any case, this did not solve the problem of the gaps between one area and another. The answer found in Britain and some other European countries was to build toll or turnpike roads along major routes. Travellers paid a small fee at toll-houses positioned every few kilometres. The fees were intended to be used to maintain the roads, but they often went into the

and this sparked off a new interest in methods of road building. It would have been too costly to copy Roman methods, but in 1764, a Frenchman, Pierre Tresaguet (1716–96), came up with a plan based on Roman ideas but much easier and cheaper to build. His roads were no more than 25 centimetres thick. The base was a closely-packed layer of large, flat stones. This was covered with a layer of much smaller, broken stones to give a smooth surface. To ensure that surface water drained off the roads, they were given a cambered top so that the middle was about 15 centimetres higher than the sides.

NEW ROADS FOR EUROPE

Tresaguet's first road was built from Paris to Toulouse, and onwards to the border with Spain. It was so successful that his road-building system was adopted in

John McAdam and Thomas Telford pioneered new road-building methods in the eighteenth century.

pockets of the collectors. Even if this did not happen, the people responsible for keeping the roads in good repair often had no idea how to do their job.

The bad state of the roads became a serious problem for traders and travellers,

many countries of Europe. It was copied in Britain by John Metcalf (1717–1810), who built 300 kilometres of roads in the north of England. He improved on Tresaguet's ideas by adding a ditch on each side of a road to give extra drainage.

ROAD SURFACES

A good road must be built on a solid base to provide support for the weight of passing vehicles.

McAdam's roads had a cambered foundation with two ten-centimetre courses of stones covered by a top layer of fine stones, and a drainage ditch at each side.

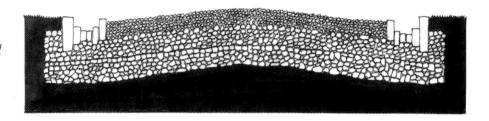

Tresaguet's roads were supported on a layer of heavy stones pushed into a stone base. Above this were two layers of smaller stones. Retaining stones at the sides kept everything in place.

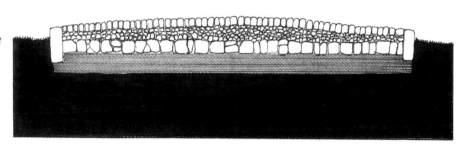

Many modern roads have a bottom layer of small stones followed by a layer of concrete, topped with a layer of tar or asphalt and another layer of asphalt above. Some have a hard shoulder with a shallow concrete foundation not designed for hard wear.

Two other British engineers made advances in the science of road-building in the early nineteenth century. They were Thomas Telford (1757–1834) and John McAdam (1756–1836). Both had the idea that the wheels of passing traffic could help to make a smooth surface for a new road by pounding the top layer into fine dust. This dust worked its way downwards to the lower layers and helped to bind them together. Telford's roads had a top layer of small stones thinly covered with gravel. McAdam's roads also had a layer of small stones on the surface, but lime was added to the stone dust to make a cement-like finish.

Roads built in this way were cheap to make and the surface was adequate for fairly slow-moving, horse-drawn transport. However, they were often damaged by rainstorms or deep frosts.

However, while Telford and McAdam were building their roads, a new form of transport was emerging. The railways were soon in command of most passenger and goods traffic, and interest in road building faded. Few new roads were built for the rest of the nineteenth century.

THE ROAD REVIVAL

The invention of petrol and diesel engines tipped the balance once more in favour of roads. Faster-moving, rubber-tyred vehicles loosened the stones of the old roads and created clouds of dust. The answer was found to be a top dressing of

ROADS

△ From about 1650 onwards, turnpikes (or toll gates) were set up at intervals along major highways to collect money (a toll) from the users of that section of road. This money was then used to improve the road's quality.

tar which sealed the dust in and evened out bumps. In the 1900s, roads began to take on their modern appearance.
As road traffic grew in the 1920s and 1930s, the old roads, even with their new tar surfaces, proved to be inadequate.

Some were too narrow. Others had bridges that needed to be strengthened, or bends that were too tight to be taken safely at speed. Many of the gradients were too steep for safety. New roads were needed, designed for the heavy, fast-moving traffic of the motor age.

HIGH-SPEED TRAFFIC
Most countries began large road-building programmes in the 1930s. The USA built

federal highways covering major routes, backed up with interstate highways. Germany called its new roads *autobahnen*. France built its *routes nationales* and Italy its *autostrada*. Britain was late starting its new road network, not opening its first motorway until 1959.

These new roads all had similar features. They separated traffic moving in different directions, and each carriageway had a number of lanes. Sharp bends and steep gradients were avoided, and careful signposting prepared drivers for road junctions. Tunnels or flyovers carried the new roads under or over city streets, and roadside verges and embankments were landscaped to give drivers a good view ahead. Ring roads and bypasses were built around major cities so that through traffic could avoid the congested city streets. Roads are once again vitally important to our everyday lives.

BUILDING TO LAST

Once they had mastered the art of working in stone, builders could build magnificent temples, palaces and tombs, designed to last for eternity.

Today, travellers visiting different corners of the globe see magnificent evidence of past lives, from the pyramids of ancient Egypt on the banks of the Nile, to the ornately carved temples of ancient Greece and Rome, and the lofty medieval cathedrals with spires soaring into the sky. These buildings, some of them thousands of years old, all have one thing in common. They are built of stone.

People had seen the usefulness of stone from earliest times. However, making small tools from pieces of flint is a very different matter to make a stone house, let alone a huge building. The small pieces of stone that people found on the ground were no good for building. A stone structure has to be made from large blocks cut to a suitable shape for fitting together. This meant quarrying

△ *Sometimes ancient quarrymen used wood wedges to cut stone from a rock face. These wedges were driven into the stone and then water was poured over them. As the wedges became wet, they expanded and cracked the stone in two.*

stone from a rock face, taking the blocks to the building site and then cutting them to shape. Attempting these tasks with simple tools must have seemed almost impossible.

MALTA'S MYSTERIOUS TEMPLES

Early civilizations left very little evidence to show how they tackled the problems of using stone. In some cases, archaeologists have been able to work out what must have happened by studying the remains of buildings. In other cases, there is so little to go on that they cannot even do this.

In about 3600 BC, people living on Malta built amazing stone temples at Tarxien, Hal Saflieni and other places on the island. These temples are not like any other buildings of the ancient world. They have separate rooms linked by passages. Each room is divided into a pair of semi-circular chambers. The walls of these strange temples are made from massive stones or 'megaliths'. Some of the temple walls are eight metres high.

The people who built these extraordinary temples disappeared without trace and left no evidence of how they worked. However they managed it, their achievement was remarkable.

▷Stones sometimes had to be dragged for long distances from the quarry to the site. Some of the stones used to build Stonehenge in Wiltshire, England, were dragged from the mountains of Wales, over 200 kilometres away.

PYRAMIDS ALONG THE NILE

Stone was not used extensively at the time the Maltese temples were built. It was to be another thousand years before a much more famous civilization began to build in stone. The pyramids were built between 2700 and 1700 BC as tombs for the pharaohs of ancient Egypt. They tell us a great deal about how the early stone-workers managed with simple tools. Although the Egyptians did not leave much written evidence about their methods, archaeologists have worked out how they could have been built.

The easiest way to transport large quantities of stone was along the river, which may be one reason why the pyramids stand near the banks of the Nile. The outer wall of the pyramid was

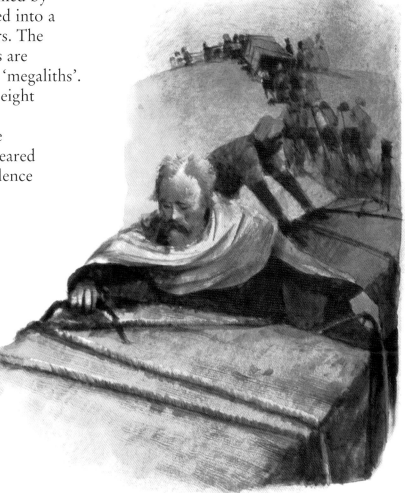

made from limestone, which was quarried at Tura, on the eastern bank of the river. Limestone is a soft rock which is easy to cut. The Egyptians had copper chisels and sharp saws to remove the stone in large blocks.

The inner core of the pyramid was granite, which probably came from Aswan in the south of Egypt. Granite is a very hard rock which would have blunted the Egyptians' copper tools when they tried to cut it. Archaeologists are not certain what method was used, but the Egyptians did somehow manage to cut the large blocks they needed. These massive blocks of stone, weighing between two and 50 tonnes, were loaded on to boats. The blocks then had to be taken from the boat to the site of the pyramid. First, a stone causeway was built from the river to the site. The blocks were loaded on to sledges and dragged up the causeway. The next problem was lifting the blocks to the necessary height. The stones were probably hauled up ramps of stone or packed mud which were specially built for the purpose. The ramps would have to be extended as the pyramid grew taller. These ramps were dismantled when the pyramid was complete.

BUILDING IN THE AMERICAS

The building of the pyramids was the first time a civilization had undertaken such a massive project, with careful planning and a huge work-force. Other civilizations also built impressive temples, palaces and tombs using simple tools. The great civilizations of Central and South America – like the Maya, the Aztecs and the Incas – ruled their empires

at a much later date than the Egyptians, but their way of life was no more sophisticated. Many of their buildings were destroyed by the Spanish conquistadors who invaded Central and South America in the sixteenth century.

▷ *It has been estimated that it took 50,000 people 20 years to build the Great Pyramid at Giza.*

The Maya people lived in the Yucatán peninsula of Mexico between AD 300 and 900. Their temples were pyramids or smaller rectangular buildings covered with elaborate carvings. In Egyptian pyramids, the stones were held in place by their own great weight. The Mayans learned to use mortar to hold the stones of their buildings together. They were the earliest American civilization to do this. They also built columns and pillars, and designed a type of arch.

The Aztecs, who ruled over a huge empire in Mexico between 1350 and 1521, built their magnificent city of Tenochtitlán on an island in a lake. Nothing remains of Tenochtitlán today and Mexico City now stands on the site. At the height of the Aztecs' power, however, about 200,000 people lived there, making it one of the largest cities in the world at the time.

The houses of farmers and craft-workers were made of wattle and daub or mud bricks, but the nobility had fine villas built of stone. Aztec temples were solid pyramids covered with mud bricks or stone. The great temple in the centre of Tenochtitlán was 150 metres high. The walls were decorated with sculptures and paintings and two steep flights of steps led up the outside to the top of the pyramid.

THE LOST CITY

The Incas had a great empire in Peru at about the same time as the Aztecs ruled in Mexico. They built fine cities such as Cuzco and Vilcabamba, but one of the most intriguing is the 'lost city' of Machu Picchu. For centuries, no one knew about Machu Picchu because there was no mention of it in the histories of the Spanish invaders. However, legends about a mysterious Inca city in the mountains led to a search, and the ruins of Machu Picchu were discovered in 1911, on a mountain ridge high in the Andes.

All the houses, palaces and temples are built from granite cut so precisely that the stones fitted together without mortar. This must have been done with stone hammers and perhaps chisels made of bronze, similar to the tools used by the Egyptians 3,000 years earlier. The buildings are at different levels on the steep mountainside, linked by more than 100 stairways, some with 150 steps.

Some of the most amazing buildings built in the past are still standing today.

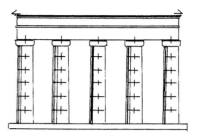

The Parthenon (top) which stands on the Acropolis in Athens, Greece, is a typical example of a Greek temple. Massive lintels are held up by rows of carved pillars. The roof would originally have been tiled. The stones of the columns were held together with iron rods.

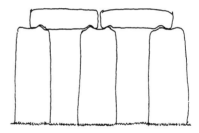

The stone circle known as Stonehenge (centre) was built between 2500 and 1500 BC. The horizontal lintels are fixed to the standing stones with 'mortise and tenon' joints. Projecting tenons on the uprights fit into holes called mortises in the lintels.

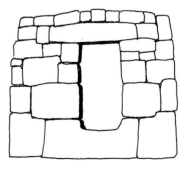

The city of Machu Picchu (bottom) gives us valuable evidence about Inca building styles. The Incas cut their stones so accurately that they fitted together without mortar.

THE TEMPLES OF GREECE AND ROME

Meanwhile, in Europe, buildings were becoming much more sophisticated. At the height of ancient Greek civilization, between 500 and 400 BC, the Greeks were using blocks of marble or limestone for their temples and public buildings. Some stones were cut so accurately that they fitted together perfectly, but the Greeks also used iron or bronze clamps to hold stones together. Columns were made by standing shaped pieces of stone on top of

each other. The stones were lifted into position with pulleys and fixed together with iron rods or wooden pegs.

The Romans were skilled engineers and they had various methods of building. The simplest was to fix regular blocks of stone together with mortar or clamps. However, one of their most important contributions to architecture was the use of concrete. Many Roman buildings had concrete walls covered with stone or bricks. One advantage of this method was

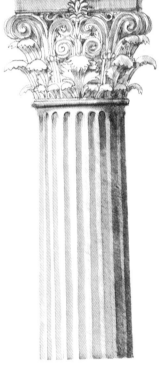

◁ The great buildings of Egypt, Greece and Rome were often decorated with carvings, sculptures and paintings. Stone was a good material for carving and artists could create religious or heroic scenes, or simply portray everyday life in their work.

that concrete walls could be built by unskilled labour, leaving the stonemasons free to carry out the more skilled and decorative work.

BUILDING IN CURVES

Until Roman times, most buildings had straight walls supporting a flat or sloping roof. The roof could be supported by the walls themselves, as in the Mediterranean mud-brick houses. It could also be supported by a wooden framework of

△ The Greeks developed three styles of column decoration. The Doric style (left) had a plain, square slab at the top. The Ionic style (centre) was more slender, with a scroll design on the top or 'capital'. In the Corinthian style (right) the capitals were larger and more decorative.

vertical and horizontal poles, as in wattle and daub structures, or by stone columns as in Greek architecture. Whichever method was used, the shapes within the building were basically flat and rectangular.

BUILDING IN CONCRETE

A concrete wall was built by making a wooden mould, called a 'form', and pouring concrete into it. When the concrete had set hard, the form was removed.

The great advantage of concrete was its strength. The Romans made their concrete by mixing small pieces of stone with a mortar of lime and sand. The mixture was easy to work, which allowed the Romans to experiment with new shapes in building, such as arches, vaults and domes.

People had made simple domed roofs long before the Romans, using a method called 'corbelling'. When the builder reached the top of the wall, he laid a row of bricks or stones that jutted slightly into the inside of the building. The next row of stones overlapped a bit more and so on until the stones met in the middle to form a roof. In a rectangular building, the roof was a simple vault. In a square building, the roof was a simple dome.

The Mycenaeans, who lived in Greece around 1300 BC, built underground domed tombs which can still be seen today. The most famous of these tombs is known as the Treasury of Atreus. It has a corbelled dome made from 34 rows or 'courses' of stone. The stones were carefully cut so that they formed a curved ceiling surface when they were laid on top of each other.

THE ARCH

The Mycenean system of corbelling could only be used for fairly small structures. It was the Romans who came up with a scheme for using domes and vaults on a larger scale. The design of many Roman buildings followed the Greek ideas, but the Romans were also influenced by the Etruscans who ruled over central Italy from 800 to 200 BC. One idea which the Romans adopted from Etruscan building was the arch. The arch is a very strong shape, good for supporting a heavy roof.

The walls of the circular Colosseum in Rome are made up of a line of arches. These were built around semi-circular wooden frames.

◁ *The Treasury of Atreus.*

▷ *The coffered ceiling of the Pantheon in Rome gives the dome a light and airy appearance. The dome is supported by buttresses.*

0   10   20   30 meters

The top stone, or 'keystone' was put in last. The arch also allowed the Romans to build strong bridges such as the Pons Fabricius in Rome.

By combining the arch with their use of concrete, the Romans began to make vaulted roofs. The simplest style was the 'barrel vault'. This fitted over a rectangular building with an arch at either end. When the walls and arches had been built, a wooden mould in the shape of the vault was fitted on top of them. Concrete was poured into the mould and left to set. Then the wooden framework was removed. The barrel vault was not just used on rectangular buildings. It could be adapted to suit buildings of different shapes. For example, a square building could be roofed with an intersecting vault made up of two barrel vaults in the shape of a cross.

SUPPORTING A DOME

The Romans also used concrete to help them build domes. One of their most famous domed buildings is the Pantheon in Rome. This circular temple is roofed with a massive concrete dome over 40 metres in diameter. One problem that the builders had to overcome was how to support such a big and heavy dome. They solved this by building the temple walls of solid concrete with an outer shell, or 'facing', of brick.

1 Barrel vault
The simplest type of vault is the barrel vault. It is shaped like half a cylinder. Building the vault is like building arches one after another along the length of the building. A barrel vault is suitable for roofing a rectangular building with an arch at each end. It is not so good for wide buildings because the height of the vault has to be increased with the width. The Romans covered their barrel vaults with concrete for a smooth finish.

2 Intersecting vault
This is made by building two barrel vaults at right angles to each other. The points where the vaults join is shaped like an 'X'. The intersecting vault is useful for roofing square buildings or parts of buildings.

3 Gothic ribbed vault
Barrel vaults were heavy and needed thick walls for support. A strong wooden frame also had to be made for support while it was being built. Stonemasons designed the ribbed vault in which strong stone 'ribs' take some of the strain. They also used pointed arches instead of round ones. This helped to add height to the vault without increasing the width of the arch.

More ribs
Gothic masons realized that they could use more ribs to provide an even stronger support and to give a more ornamental appearance at the same time. The intricately patterned ceilings of medieval churches and cathedrals are some of the most beautiful in the world.

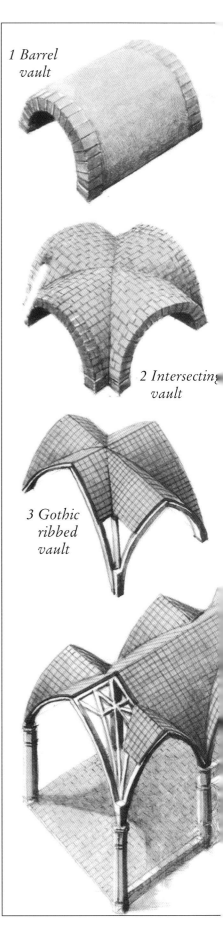

1 Barrel vault

2 Intersecting vault

3 Gothic ribbed vault

GOTHIC ARCHITECTURE

Gothic architecture flourished in Europe between the twelfth and fifteenth centuries, mainly in the building of churches and cathedrals. Its main features are ribbed ceilings, pointed arches and flying buttresses.

The elegant flying buttresses (4), joined the wall at the top of their arches, helping to spread the weight of the vaulted roof over a wider area.

A wooden framework (5) was built over the vaulted stone ceiling to support the outer roof.

△ A large number of people were needed to work on a building such as a cathedral. Temporary wooden workshops were built on the site for working on individual items and storing equipment.

To help take the strain of the roof, they added 'buttresses', or supports built against the walls to bear some of the weight. The dome on the Pantheon was made lighter by 'coffering' the ceiling. The dome is supported by thick concrete ribs arranged in a pattern of squares. The concrete in the centre of the squares is thinner than on the ribs.

The Romans used the Pantheon as a model for many circular buildings with domes. However, they did not achieve the next step, which was to build a dome on a square building. The first people to manage this were the Byzantines, a new civilization which rose up as the Roman Empire declined. Byzantium was the first Christian empire and the Byzantines built magnificent domed churches such as Hagia Sophia in the capital city of Constantinople (modern-day Istanbul).

BUILDINGS MADE OF LIGHT

The Middle Ages was the period of Gothic architecture in Europe. The main feature of Gothic architecture is the pointed arch. This was more elegant than the earlier, rounded Roman or Norman

BYZANTINE DOMES

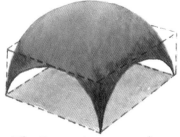

The Byzantines were the first to overcome the problem of building a dome on a square building. The problem is that a square can only support a circle in the four places where it touches.

The outer dotted lines show the diameter of a sphere fitted over the square. Arches would need to be cut in the sphere so that it did not overlap the square. The wall would then be built up to the top of arches, giving a very shallow dome.

The Byzantine answer was to split the design in two. Arches were formed by curved wedges on each corner. These were supported on massive stone pillars or piers.

The curved stonework met to leave an open circle that the dome could rest on. The dome could be much higher and the piers and arches would support the weight.

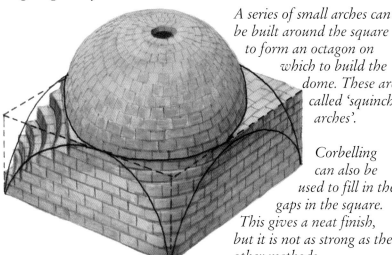

A series of small arches can be built around the square to form an octagon on which to build the dome. These are called 'squinch arches'.

Corbelling can also be used to fill in the gaps in the square. This gives a neat finish, but it is not as strong as the other methods.

BRIDGES

Building bridges was not easy before the development of the arch. A narrow stream could be bridged with a log but a bridge across a wider gap had to be supported from below. Early bridges were built by supporting flat stone slabs on a row of stone pillars or piers set in the river bed. This only worked if the river was fairly narrow and shallow enough to build the piers. Once the Romans realized that arches could be used to build bridges, wider rivers could be spanned. The Romans built bridges with a series of semi-circular arches which cut down on the number of piers needed to support the bridge.

The Chinese were the first to use a shallow arch which could span a wide gap without going too high. The Great Stone Bridge over the River Chiao Shui in China (below) looks very modern even though it was built in AD 610. It has a shallow arch with a span of 37.5 metres. Many modern bridges have a similar shallow arch.

arch and it also allowed the roof to be vaulted in different ways. The soaring, vaulted roofs of medieval cathedrals were built using stone ribs to support the ceiling above tall, pointed arches. The places where the ribs met on the ceiling were hidden by carvings called 'bosses'.

The tall, graceful arches, large windows and high, delicate ceilings gave these buildings a light and airy appearance which had not been possible before. As stonemasons realized what beautiful effects they could create, the patterns of ribs and bosses grew more and more elaborate and decorative.

Gothic stonemasons needed to find a way to support the weight of the heavy stone roofs of the cathedrals. They came up with 'flying buttresses', shaped like arches, but detached from the wall at ground level and curving in to meet it higher up.

From the Egyptian pyramids to the European cathedrals, amazing stone buildings have been designed to last for eternity in celebration of gods and kings. All over the world, examples of the work of early builders still stand today as monuments to their great skill and have had an influence on architecture ever since.

METAL FRAMES

For thousands of years, buildings were made of brick, stone and wood. Then, about 200 years ago, architects began to use metal frames to revolutionize building methods and designs, shaping the city skylines of today.

n 1779, there was only one talking-point among people in the village of Coalbrookdale in Shropshire, England. Nearby, where the main road crossed the River Severn, a new bridge was being built. Its one arch crossed the river in a single span of 30 metres. What made the bridge unusual was that it was built entirely of iron, the first of its kind in the world. Wood or stone were the usual bridge-building materials. People wondered if the iron bridge would be safe, especially as it would carry heavy coal wagons. These worries increased when they heard that

the bridge would be held together, not by nuts and bolts, but by a system of wedges.

THE BRIDGE HOLDS

Abraham Darby III (1750–89), grandson of the first man to make cast iron in England, built the iron bridge, and proved the critics wrong. The bridge held firm, and is still there today. Darby had

△ *The Crystal Palace, scene of Great Britain's 'Great Exhibition' of 1851, was built of cast-iron pillars and thousands of sheets of glass.*

△ The iron bridge at Coalbrookdale became so famous that the town around it was renamed 'Ironbridge'.

shown that iron was an ideal material for building large structures. His bridge started a building revolution.

The bridge at Coalbrookdale was the first of many. Among those who were impressed with it was a Scottish engineer, Thomas Telford (1757–1834). In 1795, when he came to build the Pont Cysyllte Aqueduct in North Wales to carry a canal across a wide valley, he chose a trough of cast iron plates, bolted together and mounted on stone piers, to take the flow of water.

Telford chose iron again when, in 1802, he submitted a design for a new London Bridge. This would have crossed the water in a single iron span of 183 metres. Telford's design was not chosen, but it was a pointer to what was possible.

THE IRON PALACE

At the beginning of the nineteenth century, there was a great enthusiasm for the new material. If cast iron could be used for bridges, why shouldn't it be used in buildings? In 1802, when the architect

METAL FRAMES

James Wyatt (1746–1813) designed a new palace at Kew, near London, for King George III (1738–1820), he included iron in the structure. Around the same time another British architect, John Nash (1752–1835), rebuilt a house in Brighton belonging to the Prince Regent, the future King George IV (1762–1830). In the Brighton Pavilion, which you can visit, he included iron staircases and iron columns to hold up the roofs of the larger rooms. These columns were disguised as the trunks of huge palm trees. Other designers began to use iron to support the balconies of churches.

▽ *The huge machines used in the manufacture of textiles needed to be housed in enormous rooms with high ceilings. Iron could provide the ideal skeletons for such buildings.*

THE I-BEAM

In the early days of building with iron, much thought was given to the best way of shaping girders to give the greatest strength combined with the lightest possible weight.

In 1850, the Britannia Bridge across the Menai Strait in North Wales was opened. It was built of rectangular iron tubes designed by a Scottish engineer and shipbuilder, William Fairbairn (1789–1874). However, rectangular tubes were expensive and heavy, so engineers worked on a cheaper and lighter alternative.

The solution was the 'I-beam', sometimes called an I-girder or plate-girder, with its upright piece longer than the head and tail pieces. This gave the necessary rigidity and strength for building. I-beams were widely used in buildings by the late nineteenth century.

METAL FRAMES

▷ *The glass and iron structure of the Crystal Palace in London was a revolutionary design.*

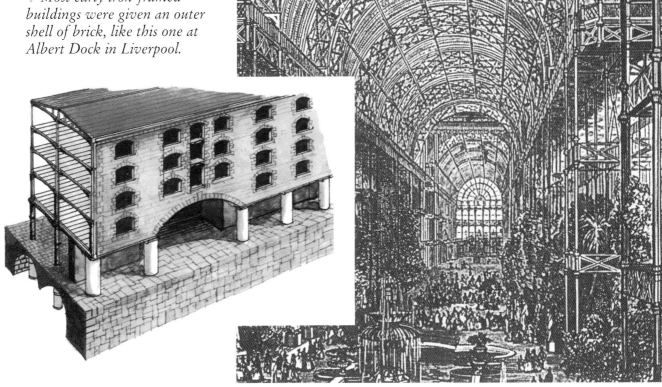

▽ *Most early iron-framed buildings were given an outer shell of brick, like this one at Albert Dock in Liverpool.*

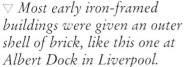

IRON FACTORIES

Before long, industry too began to make use of the new iron-framed buildings. The large, new spinning and weaving machines which were coming into use at this time were operated by belts from an overhead shaft usually driven by steam, and demanded huge, open floor areas for production and storage.

They also needed to be housed in buildings with several storeys to make the maximum use of space. A system of cast iron pillars and beams creating spacious, open rooms was the perfect answer.

The first factory to be built in this way was a spinning mill at Shrewsbury in England, opened in the 1790s. This example was quickly copied, although the cast iron frames were usually disguised to look like stone.

James Watt (1738–1819), whose development of the steam engine had brought about a revolution in industry, became interested in building factories from cast iron parts made in his own factory. One factory he designed, a mill built at Salford near Manchester in 1801, was the first to use I-shaped beams. These are now standard components of large building structures.

BUILDING IN A FRAME

So far, cast iron had only been used as part of the internal structure of buildings. Stone or brick walls were still used for the outward appearance of the buildings and to help support floors and roofs. The next step was to use a metal frame for the outside of the building and let it take all the weight. For the outside walls, the frame could then be filled in with a lighter material such as metal sheets or glass.

One of the pioneers in this kind of building was an American, James Bogardus (1800–74). He became interested in architecture after inventing a wide variety of small devices ranging from engraving machines to gas meters. In 1847, Bogardus built his own five-storey factory in New York which was the first cast iron building in the United States. He went on to build many others, using standard-sized parts which could be assembled in a variety of different ways. These were the first mass-produced buildings.

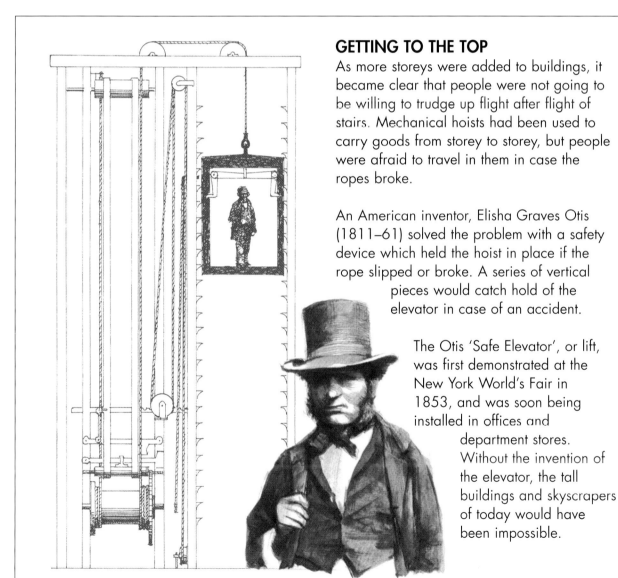

GETTING TO THE TOP

As more storeys were added to buildings, it became clear that people were not going to be willing to trudge up flight after flight of stairs. Mechanical hoists had been used to carry goods from storey to storey, but people were afraid to travel in them in case the ropes broke.

An American inventor, Elisha Graves Otis (1811–61) solved the problem with a safety device which held the hoist in place if the rope slipped or broke. A series of vertical pieces would catch hold of the elevator in case of an accident.

The Otis 'Safe Elevator', or lift, was first demonstrated at the New York World's Fair in 1853, and was soon being installed in offices and department stores. Without the invention of the elevator, the tall buildings and skyscrapers of today would have been impossible.

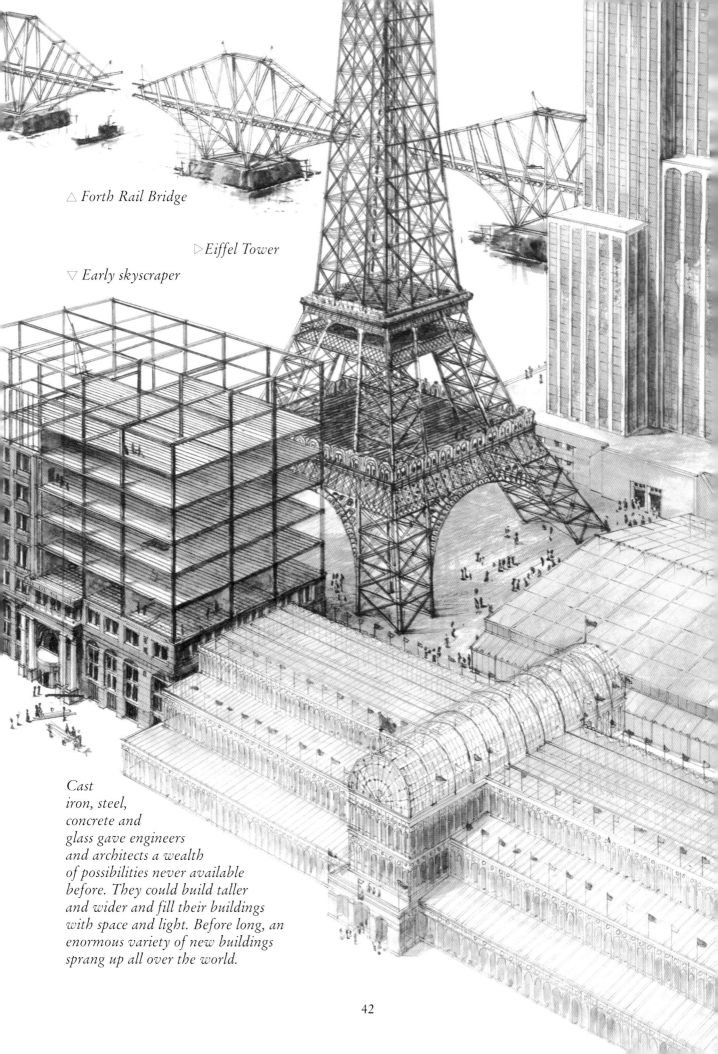

△ *Forth Rail Bridge*

▷*Eiffel Tower*

▽ *Early skyscraper*

*Cast
iron, steel,
concrete and
glass gave engineers
and architects a wealth
of possibilities never available
before. They could build taller
and wider and fill their buildings
with space and light. Before long, an
enormous variety of new buildings
sprang up all over the world.*

42

◁ *Empire State Building*

◁ *Palais des Machines*

◁ *Crystal Palace*

THE RAILWAY AGE

Meanwhile, in Europe, there were other developments. The railways had created a need for large buildings, especially at city stations. Cast iron structures were ideal. One of the first of these large stations to be built was at Paddington in London. It was jointly designed by Isambard Kingdom Brunel (1806–59) and Matthew Digby Wyatt (1820–77), and opened in 1854. With a graceful three-arched iron-and-glass roof supported on slim pillars, it spanned 73 metres.

The design of Paddington station was influenced by an even more dramatic building which had arisen in London in 1851. This was the year of the Great Exhibition, which was to be a showplace for all the products of the British Empire. To house it, a vast glass and iron building, known as the Crystal Palace, was erected in London's Hyde Park.

The Crystal Palace was designed by Joseph Paxton (1801–65), who had started his working life as a gardener. This had led him to build iron and glass greenhouses, and it was on these that he based his design for the Crystal Palace. As the centrepiece for an exhibition which was acclaimed worldwide, it brought valuable publicity for the techniques of metal construction. The Crystal Palace remained in the public eye for 85 years. When the Great Exhibition was over, the building was moved to south London as a concert hall and exhibition centre. It remained a landmark until it burned down in 1936.

THE GREAT TOWER OF PARIS

Another great European exhibition, the Paris Exhibition of 1889, provided two more striking examples of iron buildings. One, the Eiffel Tower, is still one of the most famous. Gustave Eiffel (1832–1923) had designed iron railway bridges and station buildings before he was asked to design a centrepiece for the Exhibition. The result was a tower 300 metres high, then the tallest building in the world. It was built of 12,000 factory-made parts which were all numbered before being put into place. Although there were fears about the Eiffel Tower's safety in high winds, as well as a great deal of criticism of its appearance, it was to become a much-loved feature of the Paris skyline.

The second great iron building at the Paris Exhibition was an exhibition hall, the Palais des Machines. This was another glass-walled and glass-roofed building, 420 metres long.

ROLLED STEEL GIRDERS

Cast iron as a building material was by now giving way to rolled steel, which was stronger and more resistant to rust. The first rolled steel girders for building were produced in England in 1855. At first, steel girders were expensive and added hugely to the cost of building, but improved production methods lowered

the price. The use of steel girders was given a boost when they were chosen for the 1,624-metre Forth Railway Bridge in Scotland, built between 1880 and 1890.

In the United States, architects adopted steel frames with enthusiasm for the building of the first skyscrapers. The Home Insurance Building in Chicago, USA, finished in 1885, was the world's first skyscraper, although today, with only ten storeys, it looks more like a model of the real thing. It had a 'skin' of thin stone walls built round a framework of cast iron columns and steel girders.

Skyscrapers became particularly popular in the USA because of the shortage of land in the cities. By 1910, there were more than 90 buildings in New York and Chicago with more than ten storeys. By 1920, the number had grown to 450.

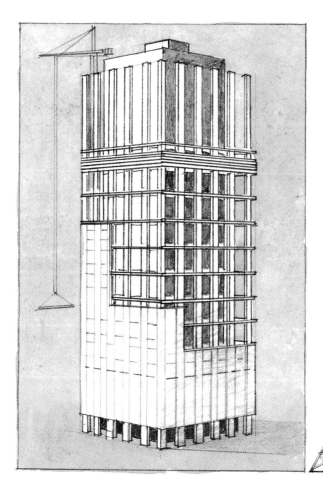

▷ *There are two main ways of building a skyscraper. Using cranes, it is built one floor at a time; using jacks, floors are assembled at ground level and then hauled into position.*

▷ *Seven of the world's tallest buildings (from far right to left):*
1 CN Tower, Toronto, Canada (1975), 550 metres
2 Sears Tower, Chicago, USA (1974), 443 metres
3 World Trade Centre, New York, USA (1973; destroyed 2001), 412 metres
4 Empire State Building, New York, USA (1931), 381 metres
5 Standard Oil Building, Chicago, USA (1973), 346 metres
6 John Hancock Building, Chicago, USA (1968), 343 metres
7 Eiffel Tower, Paris, France (1889; extended 1959) to 321 metres

HIGHER AND HIGHER

Meanwhile, yet another type of construction was becoming popular. This was reinforced concrete, which was liquid concrete poured over steel rods. The first large steel-and-concrete skyscraper was the Woolworth Building in New York, completed in 1913 and designed by Cass Gilbert (1859–1934). It had 52 storeys and rose to a height of 242 metres. Of all the buildings in the world at the time, only the Eiffel Tower was taller.

However, the Woolworth Building held the record only until 1931, when New York's Empire State Building, 381 metres high, was opened. In 1974, the record fell again to the Sears Tower in Chicago, which is 443 metres.

The Woolworth Building, with its pencil-like tower rising through the sky, was a milestone in architecture. From then on, city skylines in America, and later throughout the world, would feature the towers of steel-framed skyscraper office blocks, hotels and apartments, competing in their height and splendour with all the descendants of Abraham Darby's innovative iron bridge in Shropshire.

FIND OUT SOME MORE

After you have read about the ideas and inventions in this book, you may want to find out some more information about them. There are lots of books devoted to specific topics, such as bridges or skyscrapers, so that you can discover more facts. All over Britain and Ireland, you can see historical sites and visit museums that contain historical artefacts that will tell you more about the subjects that interest you. The books, sites and museums listed below cover some of the most important topics in this book. They are just a start!

GENERAL INFORMATION
BOOKS
These books all present a large number of inventions of all different kinds:

Oxford Illustrated Encyclopedia of Invention and Technology edited by Sir Monty Finniston (Oxford University Press, 1992)

Usborne Illustrated Handbook of Invention and Discovery by Struan Reid (Usborne, 1986)

Invention by Lionel Bender (Dorling Kindersley, 1986)

The Way Things Work by David Macaulay (Dorling Kindersley, 1988)

Key Moments in Science and Technology by Keith Wicks (Hamlyn, 1999)

A History of Invention by Trevor I. Williams (Little Brown, 1999)

WEBSITE
For information on many different inventions, visit: http://inventors.about.com

MUSEUMS
Many large museums contain interesting artefacts related to people of the past, and some have collections that may be more specifically about some of the themes covered in this book.

To find out more about the museums in your area, ask in your local library or tourist information office, or look in the telephone directory.

A useful guide is *Museums & Galleries in Great Britain & Ireland* (British Leisure Publications, East Grinstead) which tells you about over 1,300 places to visit. For a good introduction to the subjects covered in this book, visit:

Science Museum, Exhibition Road, London SW7 www.sciencemuseum.org.uk

For displays and information about many of the earliest ideas and inventions, go to:

British Museum, Great Russell Street, London WC1 www.britishmuseum.co.uk

BUILDING
BOOKS
Inside an Egyptian Pyramid by Jacqueline Morley (Simon & Schuster, 1991)

Inside a Medieval Cathedral by Fiona Macdonald (Simon & Schuster, 1991)

How They Were Built by David J Brown (Kingfisher, 1991)

Building by Philip Wilkinson (Dorling Kindersley, 1995)

SITES
You can see medieval cathedrals in Salisbury, Canterbury, Chichester, York, Ripon, Rochester, Oxford and many other cities around Britain.

Weald & Downland Open Air Museum, Singleton, near Chichester, West Sussex.
www.wealddown.co.uk
Over 30 rescued, historic buildings, including a medieval farmstead and a working watermill.

Avoncroft Museum of Historic Buildings, near Bromsgrove, Worcestershire.
www.avoncroft.co.uk
An excellent collection of rescued historic buildings.

BUILDING WITH METAL
SITES
Ironbridge & Information Centre, Telford, Shropshire.
www.ironbridge.org.uk
The famous iron bridge is still used today, and there is an iron museum containing Abraham Darby's furnace and an industrial museum too.

INDEX